SMART BITCHES
BUY BITCOIN

A Simple Guide for Women Who Want to Learn the Truth About Bitcoin and Control Their Financial Future

Branden LaNette
and Andrea Waltz

Published by

SHORT BOOKS. BIG IDEAS.

www.SuccessIn100Pages.com

ISBN 978-1-947814-54-7

Copyright © Branden LaNette & Andrea Waltz, 2021

DEDICATION:

To all the "Smart Bitches" who have already educated themselves about Bitcoin and are leading the charge toward a very exciting future for us all. Investing in Bitcoin will never be smooth sailing—choppy seas are a necessary part of the journey—but these women have taken the helm and are steering the ship toward distant, future shores.

WARNING:

Branden tends to use a bit of foul language (you know, like *fuck-this* and *fuck that*) while Andrea tends to be fairly PG-13. So, when swearing appears, you can safely assume it's Branden.

ANOTHER WARNING:

In case you skipped the small print in the book disclaimer, neither Branden nor Andrea are financial advisors. They are just two girls standing in front of a group of readers asking them to love them, and—hopefully—Bitcoin. So, listen up, bitches: NONE of the information in this book is offered as financial advice. **Do your own research. And never invest more than you can afford to lose.**

IMPORTANT CLARIFICATION:

The *Urban Dictionary* considers the word "bitch" one of the most versatile words in the English language. And, while it is sometimes used in a derogatory way (usually by men—just sayin') it can also be used to describe an empowered, assertive woman. That is the way we're using it here. In other words, when you see *bitches*, don't think female dog—think female *wolf.*

To Impact the World, This Book Requires Us (the Authors) and You (the Reader) to Keep Three Promises:

1) **WE** promise to keep things straightforward, brutally honest and really, really simple. If you were hoping for detailed explanations on hash rates, nodes, mining pools, or Merkle trees, you've come to the wrong place.

2) **YOU** promise to read the entire book, from cover to cover—multiple times if necessary—until you understand how life-changing investing in Bitcoin can be.

3) **TOGETHER,** we make sure to spread the word to other women. Five years from now, none of us want our friends and family coming to us and saying, "Hey, why in the fuck didn't you tell me about Bitcoin?"

-Branden LaNette & Andrea Waltz

Here's What We're Going to Cover, Bitches:

Introduction

Remember when the internet first came about? No one had a clue what it was. There's a famous clip of Katie Couric asking her producer during a live TV segment, "Alison, what is *internet*?" She was a talk show anchor, you'd think she'd have known. She didn't. Virtually no one did.

The same thing was true when people first heard about cellular phones. People scoffed at the idea that anyone would want one. "Why would anyone need to make a phone call from a car?"

The same thing is true about home computers and websites. Computers were for "business" and gigantic—a computer would fill an entire room. Today, just a few short decades later, 8-year-olds have phones and iPads, and many of them *design* websites.

Now, there are these new things: "blockchain technology" and "cryptocurrencies"—the most well-known of which is Bitcoin.

* * *

Admit it: when you first heard about Bitcoin, what was your reaction? You probably went through the same stages everyone goes through: Bitcoin? What's Bitcoin? Digital money for the internet? We already have money. Sounds like a scam. Sounds like a good way to lose your ass. Anyone who invests in that will be sorry.

Then, a few years later, you heard about Bitcoin again. And even though everyone you knew was talking about it, the part of you that had decided it was stupid earlier wants to be right. So, you continued to hold out.

Then one day you were watching TV and the newscaster said, "Bitcoin, which was selling for $1 per coin a few short years ago, has just hit $3,000." You realize that maybe you were wrong about Bitcoin, it looks like it's growing in acceptance. But still you do nothing—you don't know how to get some even if you wanted to.

Fast forward to today: Bitcoin (at the time of this writing) is at $60,000 per coin. People who bought it a few years ago have become millionaires. So, what do you do? If you're like most people, you shrug and tell yourself, "Well, it's too late now."

Newsflash, bitches: It's not too late (in fact, it's early.) But you gotta get your ass in gear.

*   *   *

Blockchain technology is about to have a greater impact on the world than many people realize. More than electric cars. More than robotics. Maybe even more than Artificial Intelligence. That's a big statement coming from two bitches who couldn't write computer code on a dare. But it's true.

The most important thing to understand here is that blockchain technology is going to be very disruptive. Major corporations, banking and whole government systems are about to get one hell of a makeover, whether they want it or not. A *tsunami of change* unlike anything the world has ever seen. This is not hyperbole.

You think the internet changed things? Just wait.

But, beware: As a result of all this change, some extremely powerful people are going to get very, very pissed. Because the system they depend on for syphoning the world's wealth to their benefit is about to be pulled out from under them like a rug.

Good.

It's about fucking time.

"My school doesn't teach me about personal finance. I'm teaching my school about #Bitcoin and cryptocurrency."

- @MissTeenCrypto

Section One:

How We Got in the Fucked-up Financial Mess We're in Today

Chapter One

The System Is Rigged

A merica is a great country. Some would say it's exceptional. We agree. But it's also exceptionally fucked up.

One of the most fucked up things about America is the way our financial system is rigged to benefit certain people, specifically people in power and those close to them. Family. Friends. Business associates. *Cronies.*

America is not unique. Every country in the world is like this to a certain degree. There are "haves" and there are "have nots" in every country.

No matter where you live, I think we can all agree it doesn't feel fair. It's demoralizing. And infuriating.

Inequality sucks.

Okay, so what are we going to do about it? The answer is most likely nothing.

One of our favorite movies is, *Liar Liar*, staring Jim Carrey. In one of the funniest scenes, the main character, Fletcher—played by Carrey—goes to retrieve his car from an impound lot, only to discover it has a big scratch. *"Hey, you scratched my car!"* Fletcher exclaims.

The impound worker responds, *"Where?"*

Fletcher points and says, *"Right there!"*

The impound guy shrugs and says, *"Oh, that was already there."*

Fletcher is incensed. *"You liar! You know what I'm going to do about this?"*

"What?" the impound guy asks.

Fletcher's reply is classic. *"Nothing!"* he declares. *"Because if I take it to small claims court, it will just drain eight hours out of my life and you probably won't show up, and even if I got the judgment, you'd just stiff me anyway. So, what I'm gonna do is piss and moan like an impotent jerk and then bend over and take it up the tailpipe!"*

The impound guy responds in a deadpan voice: *"You've been here before, haven't ya?"*

Feeling Hopeless and Helpless

That's the way we all feel when dealing with "the system"—any system—when we feel there is nothing that can be done to change it. We feel helpless and powerless. And, to a certain degree, we are. There's very little the average person can do to effect change with something as large as the banking system and/or the government.

And as if it weren't bad enough already, Covid-19 put a big exclamation point on the already-dramatic level of income inequality.

For example, since the pandemic started, the combined wealth of all U.S. billionaires increased by over $1 trillion. The wealth of the five richest billionaires (Elon Musk, Jeff Bezos, Bill Gates,

Mark Zuckerberg, and Warren Buffett) increased by a staggering 85 percent, from $358 billion to $661 billion.

We're not saying they didn't earn it, or that they don't deserve their wealth. But we are saying that during this place and time, when so many individuals and small businesses are suffering so greatly, watching the rich get richer feels like a punch to our collective gut.

The Cantillon Effect

In the 1700s, French banker and philosopher, Richard Cantillon, wrote an essay on economic theory, aptly titled "An Essay on Economic Theory." The main premise of the essay was his observation that, when governments printed money in times of economic hardship, it always passed through the hands of the rich on the way to the poor. The rich—in particular, rich bankers—got their "cut" before the money made its way to the intended recipients.

In other words, the closer someone was to the king, the more they benefitted. Worse still, not only did the rich benefit most from the money, but poor people were harmed—they ended up *worse off* than before the money was printed.

What Richard Cantillon observed 400 years ago is nothing compared to the financial benefits going to rich corporate CEOs, hedge fund managers and bankers today.

In fact, it has been calculated the bottom 50 percent of income earners will pocket just $1,228 dollars, while a person with a net worth of $2 billion will pocket (drumroll, please) $400 fucking million.

Cantillon could just as well have worked for Bloomberg, writing about what he was seeing today. And it doesn't take a rocket scientist (or French philosopher) to see the Cantillon Effect playing out right before our eyes.

In 2016, then Federal Reserve Chair, Janet Yellen, gave a speech in which she basically admitted the rich and powerful get money first, and then it makes its way to the peasants who need it. But most of it never gets there. It gets hijacked, siphoned off, and hoarded.

We are not big fans of handouts either. Handouts are, at best, temporary solutions to the problems we face. We are, at our core, believers in the free-market and "money for nothing" is generally a bad idea (as are chicks for free).

But if we are going to deliver money via helicopter, it pisses us off when the well-connected few end up with the cash intended for the disconnected many.

But the Stock Market Is Soaring!

The money "meant for everyone" is showing up big in one specific place. Where? In the stock market.

As we write these words, the stock market is soaring, having just passed 32,000. And this is great for average Americans who have money in the stock market, right? Well, yes, and no. On the surface everything looks fine, better than fine—up, up, up, with no end in sight. But that's not true. There *is* an end in sight, and the end isn't all that far away.

Most people are putting their heads in the sand and hoping everything continues, but it won't. The stock market *is* going to crash. It always does.

So, when is the market going to crash? Fuck if we know. No one knows—well, almost no one. The rich and well-connected know, not the exact date, but reasonably close. And how do they know? Simple. Because they're the ones who are crashing it.

But, as usual, by the time the market crashes, the big money players will have already pulled their money out. And even if they haven't, can you spell *bailout*?

No, when the stock market crashes, it will be the average Joe and Joan who gets crushed. And then it's bye-bye 401k. And bye-bye retirement.

Don't be lulled into believing things are okay, because they aren't. The good times we are experiencing (to the degree that we are) are an illusion.

The financial system, as we once knew it, died in 2008. What you see today is a hologram; a *smoke and mirrors* fake system propped up by money being printed by the Federal Reserve.

What Women are Taught About Investing

You might be shocked or surprised by the things we've been sharing. (And believe us, there's a lot more, too.) But unless you go out of your way to read or listen to people in the economic and financial world, most of this stuff is not frontpage news.

Sadly, most woman would rather not be burdened by dry and boring economic bullshit—until recently, us included.

Here is a detailed summary of the financial education most young women get in school while growing up:

1) _____

2) _____

3) _____

Okay, maybe we're exaggerating a bit, but chances are good the lessons you *did* learn, didn't serve you well. And if you feel you *did* receive good financial education, you're one smart bitch already. But sadly, if you are like most of us, you didn't get taught shit.

When you got your first job, maybe you opened a checking account, so you had somewhere to put your sad excuse for a paycheck. And somewhere along the way, you got a credit card. That was a fucking amazing day.

But then you got the statement where you learned there was a "limit," they charged you "interest," *and* you needed to pay it down so you could keep using it. You learned how to pay rent, the electric bill, and the cable bill. You probably got wise to fees. Fees for not paying on time. Fees for having too little money. Fees for using the wrong ATM to withdraw money. Fees on top of fucking fees.

This is how most of us learned about money and finances. No wonder we did not want to learn more. That shit is depressing.

So, we didn't go out of our way to get educated and probably neither did you. Couple that with no one really tells you shit, unless they are collecting a fee, and here we are.

According to Annuity.org: *"Women are three times as likely as men to say they can't afford to save for retirement and have significantly lower rates of financial literacy. Generally speaking, women earn less, save less, and live longer—but are still responsible for the same living expenses men pay."*

This is fucked up, bitches.

We can no longer afford (literally) to allow our financial futures to be out of our hands. It's time you get some education. You must figure some shit out for yourself.

You can't afford to be ignorant. You can't afford to allow the man in your life, no matter how fabulous he may be, to do it all. And if you are the one in charge of the purse strings? Great. But you still need more education.

A Bitcoin education.

Because cutting coupons, canceling Netflix the day before it renews, and using the cheapest moisturizer at Walgreens are decent strategies but they are not enough. And it's no quality of life, either.

You need to take control.

You need to have an "investment" mentality.

"I would like to get rid of the Federal Reserve, too! I would like to have money controlled by a computer."

- Economist Milton Friedman, 1991

Chapter Two

Richard M.otherfucking Nixon

Whether he knew what he was doing or not, few people have had a greater negative impact on the U.S. dollar than President Richard M. Nixon.

The year was 1971, and with inflation on the rise, the Nixon administration felt it needed to take bold action. So "Tricky Dick," along with his top advisors, got together for a three-day sleepover at Camp David to tackle the problem. The goal? A new economic plan that would kill two birds with one stone: first, stop inflation and second, lower the unemployment rate.

Here's a bit of the conversation, recorded with a CIA-provided device hidden in Paul Volker's boxer shorts:

(Official CIA Transcript)

> Nixon: Well, boys, anyone got any ideas?
>
> Advisor #1: How about a price freeze?
>
> Nixon: What do you mean?
>
> Advisor #2: I think what ███ (redacted) is suggesting is you sign an executive order that makes price increases illegal.
>
> Nixon: Can we do that?

Advisor #1: I don't see why not. We are the
government, right?

Advisor #3: What about taking the U.S. off the gold
standard?

(sounds of unintelligible group murmuring)

Nixon: Holy crap, ▓▓▓▓▓ (redacted), that's a fine
fucking idea. That would keep those European bastards
from demanding we send them our gold. We just
disconnect the two. Genius!

Advisor #2: Well, there could be ramifications—you
know, unintended consequences.

Nixon: For example?

Advisor #2: I don't know, sir, that's why they call them
unintended consequences.

Nixon: Fuck it, let's do it. Unintended consequences be
damned.

Several days later, Nixon went on television to address the
nation and deliver the news that the United States had made a
few small changes to the monetary policy, designed to increase
prosperity, create new jobs, and halt inflation.

The immediate result of Nixon's changes: Unemployment grew
to 8.5 percent, inflation soared to 11.5 percent, and the OPEC oil
embargo made gasoline prices soar, resulting in mile-long lines
of cars at filling stations.

Fast-forward fifty years and the dollar has lost over eighty
percent of its buying power and our country has suffered twelve
major financial crises. Unintended consequences, indeed.

Today, the moves made by the Nixon administration are considered by most financial experts as some of the biggest monetary mistakes in the history of the world. Why? Because of what it did to the value of the U.S. dollar.

Taking the dollar off the gold standard meant the Federal Reserve could print as much money as they wanted, regardless of how much (or little) gold was held by the government in reserve (think *Girls Gone Wild*, but with a money press.)

Lessons from The Weimar Republic

The Weimar Republic (pronounced Vymar, which was basically Germany before Germany became Germany) was an extremely prosperous society. But during World War I, things began to turn.

From 1914 to 1919, prices of normal goods doubled. Ouch. Then, during a five-month period in 1922, prices doubled again. Double ouch.

As expected, when things began to crumble, the citizens started to grumble.

Eventually the German Central Bank, knowing it had to do something to keep its citizens happy (also known as getting them to shut up and go back to work) responded to the pressure and started printing money. The government backed the move, and for a while, things seemed better. But as with all things that seem too good to be true, it was.

The printing presses kept running, and soon prices began to rise at a dizzying rate. For example, consider this scene at a German pub:

A One-Act, Two-Beer Play

A German man walks into pub and says to the bartender:

Man: *Barkeeper, wie viel kostet ein Bier?*

  (Bartender, how much is a beer?)

Bartender: *Ein Bier kostet 8.000 Mark.*

  (A beer is 8,000 Marks.)

Man: *Gut, gieß mir ein Bier ein.*

  (Good, give me a beer.)

Five minutes passes and the man finishes his beer, then asks for another.

Man: *Barkeeper, bring mir noch eine Biere!*

  (Bartender, bring me another beer!)

The bartender draws a second beer from the tap and sets it on the bar. Five more minutes passes and, after the man downs the last of his second beer, he asks for the check:

Man: *Gib mir den Scheck.*

  (Give me my check.)

The bartender lays the check in front of the man, who takes a look at it and explodes:

Man: *Was ist das? 20.000 Mark! Sie sagten, ein Bier sei nur 8.000 Mark!*

  (What is this? 20,000 Marks! You said a beer was only 8,000 Marks.)

Bartender: *8.000 Mark das war der Preis, als Sie das erste Beir bestellten. Als Sie das zweite Bier bestellten, stieg der Pries*

auf 12,000 Mark. Das ist inflation.
Wenn Sie beide Biere zum Gleichen
Preis haben möchten, Sie sollten sie
gleichzeitig bestsllen.

(8,000 Marks was the price when you
ordered the first beer. By the time you
ordered the second beer, the price went
up to 12,000 Marks. That is inflation. If
you wanted both beers for the same
price, you should have ordered them at
the same time.)

Unfortunately, for the people of Weimar Republic, this was no
joke—it was real life.

As prices continued to soar, people started to get nervous and
began buying any tangible goods they could get their hands on—
everything from real estate to gold, from diamonds to rare
works of art. People bought things they didn't need, just so
they'd have something to barter with. Some people even started
buying pianos, even though no one in the family played. Even if
they couldn't sell it or trade it, at least they could break it up and
burn the wood for heat.

Again, in case you think we're kidding, we're not. This was life
in the Weimar Republic in the early 1920s.

They Stopped Printing Money, Right?

If this what you think—that the government saw the error of
their ways and stopped printing money—you're giving
government too much credit. No, to keep up with rising prices,
money printing was sped up. The presses ran day and night.

The problem was, now everything was so expensive, people had to take all the cash they had to the store in a wheelbarrow. To solve *that* problem, the government started printing 1 million Mark notes. Then 10 million Mark notes. Eventually a 1,000-billion Mark note came out. People would buy a loaf of bread, hand over a billion Mark note and tell the baker to keep the change.

Soon after, the Mark was worthless.

There's even a story about a man who took every Mark he owned out of the bank, put it in a wheelbarrow, and rolled the wheelbarrow to the store in hopes of buying a pound of sugar. He went inside to ask the price, leaving the wheelbarrow on the sidewalk. When he came out a minute later, he discovered someone had dumped the money on the sidewalk and had stolen the wheelbarrow.

Does any of the story about the Weimar Republic sound familiar? It should. Because what Nixon did was make the same mistakes made by the government of the Weimar Republic. We elect our leaders because we think they have some plan for taking us safely into the future, for the love of fuck. At a minimum, we expect them to avoid the mistakes of the past. Especially big ones.

(BTW: Taking the U.S. off the gold standard was supposed to be temporary. As the saying goes, there's nothing so permanent as a temporary government program.)

"Bitcoin is all about freedom of choice and I for one hope that we can see more women use it as a mechanism to create opportunities for themselves."

- Lea Thompson @girlgone_crypto

Chapter Three

Inflation: Coming Soon to a Country Near You

L augh if you want about the Weimar Republic, but if things don't change and change fast, these won't be stories about Germany a century ago—they'll be stories about daily life in America. Because we just keep printing money.

To say there has been a *surge* in the U.S. money supply is an understatement. This means inflation is coming. Lots of it. To quote Morgan Stanley: *"We have never observed money supply growth as high as it is today."*

During a three-month period in 2020, the Federal Reserve increased the U.S. money supply by almost twenty-five percent. The national debt is now over $27 trillion dollars. To put this in perspective, a trillion is a one with twelve zeros after it:

1,000,000,000,000.

If you were to place one trillion dollars in a stack, the stack would be 67,866 miles high, almost three times around the Earth at its equator.

We're on a financial Titanic, and we'd better be putting our life vests on because pretty soon we may be clinging to a fucking wooden door next to Leonardo DiCaprio, looking up and wondering why that bitch, Kate Winslet, isn't helping us out of the water.

Inflation Defined in Seven Words

Inflation is not a difficult concept to understand. In fact, it can be summed up in just seven words:

"Too much money chasing too few goods."

Suppose your favorite band, *The Trailer Park Popsicles*, are coming to town, and you want to go see them in concert. (You remember concerts, right, where people used to go see bands live, in a stadium?) But then you hear there is only going to be one show, and everyone wants to go. Yikes!

Right off the bat, you know tickets are going to be hard to get, so ticket prices will be through the roof. Worse still, you want to sit in the first three rows so you can catch the eye of the extremely hot lead guitarist. This means there's only one hundred tickets or so. Getting a ticket was going to be hard enough, but in the first few rows? You might need to go to a scalper.

Summary: Too much money chasing too few tickets.

Now, say it comes out that the lead singer isn't going to be there. He's taking a month away from the tour due to "exhaustion" (translation: he's in rehab) so the band is going to perform without him. Screw that! You're not going. Everyone feels the same way, now no one wants to go. They've got so many unsold tickets that the local radio station is giving them away for free to the 23rd caller, but no one is calling.

Summary: Too little money chasing too many tickets.

In a nutshell, that's supply and demand, and it describes inflation perfectly.

The Dollar has Been Decimated

Inflation has already taken its toll on the U.S. dollar, only no one has noticed because the erosion has been gradual. How much value has the dollar lost? The graph below shows the loss of buying power over the last one hundred years:

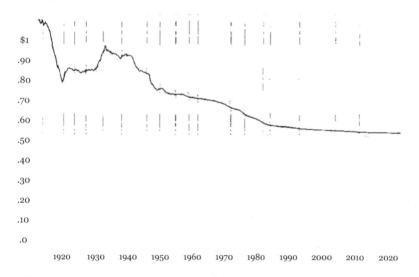

In the last 100 years, it has lost 95 percent of its buying power, and that's with just 1-2 percent inflation per year.

But now, the Federal Reserve has been printing money like they own a printing press (which they do), and the government has been throwing that money around like candy from a parade float.

Most recently they've been printing money in the name of "stimulus." As Max Keiser and Stacy Herbert often say on their Orange Pill Podcast, *"Money printer go burrrrrrrrrrrrrrr."*

Five minutes ago, you probably thought printing money was a good thing. Now you know it's not, because the more they print, the more prices on everything go up.

Mo' money, mo' inflation.

We might even be entering an era of hyper-inflation. What's the difference?

- Inflation means the cost of a loaf of bread goes from $3 to $3.50. Not good, but survivable.

- Hyperinflation means the price of a loaf of bread goes from $3 to $30.

Can you spell Weimar Republic?

When is Hyperinflation Going to Hit?

We know what you're thinking—none of this is possible, not here in America.

No one thinks it's going to happen in *their* country. But it can. Just ask the people of Venezuela. And Zimbabwe. And Cyprus. Or Argentina. Or Greece. None of them saw it coming, or if they did, they looked the other way. If you don't see it, maybe you're not looking. Time to get your head out of your mask.

Hyperinflation is a very real possibility.

When? We're not sure. Maybe five-to-ten years from now. Who knows, perhaps even sooner.

As Ernest Hemingway said:

Q: *"How did you go bankrupt?"*

A: *"Two ways. Gradually, then suddenly."*

That's how it's going to happen here, too. So far, it's been happening *gradually*. Prepare for *suddenly*.

You think trying to buy toilet paper during the early months of Covid was bad, just wait until supermarket shelves are completely empty. Ever see pictures of Russians shopping during the Cold War? If the Federal Reserve doesn't stop printing money, you could see it again, only the pictures won't be from Moscow—they'll be from Cincinnati.

The good news is that there is hope.

And things are about to change.

Not to society overall—income differences and income inequality will always exist. And we're not naïve enough to think the average person can change a system that is so deeply entrenched. But it *is* finally possible for the average Joe (or Joan) to escape the system and create their *own* system.

The days of bending over and taking it up the tailpipe may finally be over.

How?

Bitcoin.

Section Two:

How Bitcoin and Blockchain Technology are About to Save the World

"Here's to the crazy ones, the misfits, the rebels, the troublemakers, the round pegs in the square holes... the ones who see things differently. They're not fond of rules, and they have no respect for the status quo. You can quote them, disagree with them, glorify, or vilify them, but the only thing you can't do is ignore them because they change things. They push the human race forward, and while some may see them as the crazy ones, we see genius, because the people who are crazy enough to think that they can change the world, are the ones who do."

- Steve Jobs

Chapter Four
Rebels with a Cause

O n August 18, 2008, the domain name Bitcoin.org was registered. Ten weeks later, on October 31, 2008, a link to a white paper appeared, authored by someone named Satoshi Nakamoto. The paper was titled: *Bitcoin: A Peer-to-Peer Electronic Cash System.*

The white paper provided a solution for a variety of existing computer programming challenges relating to digital scarcity. In it, Satoshi laid out exactly how the technology would work.

So, who in the hell is Satoshi Nakamoto? That's a good question, because to this day, nobody knows. Is Satoshi a man? A woman? A group of people? Whoever Satoshi is, he/she/they wanted to remain anonymous. And, like Keiser Söze in *The Usual Suspects*, Satoshi simply disappeared.

Poof.

The first known commercial transaction took place in May 2010, when a computer programmer named Laszlo Hanyecz ordered two pizzas from Papa John's and paid in Bitcoin. The price? ฿10,000. He did it kind of as a joke since Bitcoin didn't have any significant value at the time. The joke turned out to be on Laszlo himself. Bitcoin's current value of $60,000 per coin makes those the most expensive pizzas in history.

We hope whoever took the Bitcoin as payment held them because they are now worth $580 million.

The Cypherpunks

The credit for Bitcoin doesn't belong entirely to Satoshi Nakamoto, since the concepts contained in his white paper were being worked on by a group of hobbyists and computer hackers known as the *cypherpunks.*

The cypherpunks believed the world was on a collision course with a sci-fi-like dystopian future where there would be a battle for human freedom. And where would this battleground take place? Cyberspace, of course. (No, you really can't make this stuff up.)

The cypherpunks believed the enemy in this battle would be various governments of the world who would try to take control, monitor, and censor people on the internet. Damn prophetic if you ask us.

With governments being as big as they are and with endless resources at their disposal, the cypherpunks needed a weapon to fight back with. Their weapon of choice was cryptography—you know, the world of mathematics and codebreaking. We're talking spy-agency-level shit that, for all they knew, might even be illegal. Some of it probably was.

Being deeply suspicious of both governments and central banks, they knew that for their plans to work, they would need to create some form of digital money.

The cypherpunks perceived money printing by central banks as a form of theft of people's money via the inflation such money-printing inevitably led to.

The result of their efforts led to the creation of blockchain technology and Bitcoin.

What is the Blockchain?

Without a doubt, blockchain technology is going to revolutionize the world. But what exactly is it? And how does it work?

The blockchain is a distributed ledger technology that describes a series of stored "blocks" of encrypted information, with each block connected to the next, creating a metaphorical "chain" of

blocks in cyberspace. It's transparent, democratic, decentralized, efficient, and secure.

And it's a total game changer.

As tempted as we are to get into the minutia of exactly how it works, we've decided not to take time to do it here for two reasons. First, the space it would require would fill the rest of the book, and second, anyone who wants to study the fine details should Google, "how does the blockchain work?" and you'll find 136,000,000 results. If you've got time, knock yourself out.

But for the purposes of *investing* in Bitcoin—or any of the thousands of other cryptocurrencies being developed using blockchain technology—all you need to know is that Bitcoin uses blockchain technology to do what Satoshi Nakamoto said it would do: become *a peer-to-peer electronic cash system.*

As Ron Burgundy would say, "It's a really big deal."

A Whole Lotta Disruption Going On

Throughout history, new technologies have disrupted older technologies, products, services, and sometimes entire industries. For example:

- Cars disrupted horse-drawn carriages.

- Planes disrupted railroads.

- Walmart disrupted Main Street retailers.

- Amazon disrupted independent bookstores, then virtually every other retail category.

- Google disrupted the Yellow Pages.

- The whiteboard disrupted the chalkboard; now SMART boards are disrupting whiteboards.

- Cellphones disrupted landline telephones.

- Digital photography virtually killed Kodak's film processing business overnight.

- Netflix disrupted Blockbuster and put them out of business.

- Starbucks disrupted the coffee industry.

- Uber disrupted the entire taxi industry.

- Email disrupted the U.S. Postal Service.

- Mastercard/Visa disrupted the use of cash for daily transactions.

- GPS virtually ended the sale of the Thompson Guide map books.

- The Apple iPod disrupted the Sony Walkman.

You could make the case that the internet disrupted virtually every industry in the world. Now, Bitcoin and blockchain technology is about to disrupt everything all over again, including:

- Healthcare
- Cybersecurity
- Energy management
- Online music
- Real estate
- Insurance
- Ride sharing
- Cloud storage
- Voting
- All aspects of government
- Supply chain management
- Movie streaming services
- Computer networking
- Public benefits (like the certain to be upcoming implementation of UBI/Universal Basic Income)
- Crowdfunding
- And many more

Yes, a lot of people are going to have a rude awakening, but the good news is that *smart bitches* who play their cards right can put themselves in position to benefit from all this chaos and disruption.

Whatever industry you are in will be impacted by blockchain technology in some way, large or small, especially if it deals in data or transactions of any kind. Blockchain technology is going to disrupt a whole lot of industries. But no industry is going to be more greatly impacted than banking.

Banks are in Trouble

Bankers already see the handwriting on the wall, and the handwriting says, *"We're fucked."*

The world's banking system is an imploding "death star" but our leaders can't see it, or they *can* and they're just stalling for time to wring the last few dollars out of the system and hopefully find a way to fix the fucking mess they created. But they won't—it's already too late.

Many experts suggest the blockchain will wreak the same havoc on the banking system as the internet did to the print media industry. As a result, a whole lot of pinstripe-clad, cigar-smoking bankers are about to find themselves unemployed. Imagine walking down the street and watching bank managers hanging "going out of business" signs on their doors.

Because of this, the banking world is in a quiet panic. Imagine two people playing chess, and even though the final ten moves have yet to be made, both players know how the game is going to end. For the bankers, it's going to end badly. Bitcoin will give millions of people in third world countries access to traditional banking and other financial services they've never had before. It will also allow people to send money across borders instantly and with relatively low fees. Truly a big deal for third-world countries.

End of the Middleman

Because Bitcoin is a *peer-to-peer* electronic cash system, it will eventually eliminate the middleman from virtually all digital transactions. This will save an enormous amount of wasted time and money from the systems as they now exist. For example, escrow services:

Imagine the process for buying a house. Party A wants to pay Party C $300,000 for their house. Today, that money goes from Party A to Party B (an escrow company) who holds that money (and charges a 1 percent fee for doing so) and then transfers the money to Party C.

This is just one example of a middleman being removed from a transaction and is admittedly presented here in a very simplified way, but you get the idea. Works out great for Party A and Party C, but Party B (the escrow company) has been cut out of the deal and lost their $3,000 fee for brokering the transaction.

How soon is this going to happen? Today? Tomorrow? Probably not. Probably not this year, either. But the clock is ticking. Even if it's five-to-ten years before everything plays out, it *will* play out.

"Bitcoin is a swarm of cyber hornets serving the goddess of wisdom, feeding on the fire of truth, exponentially growing ever smarter, faster, and stronger behind a wall of encrypted energy."

- Michael Saylor

Chapter Five

Gold Is Money, Cash Is Trash

The terms "money" and "currency" are often used interchangeably, as if they were the same thing. To say money and currency are the same thing because they have value, is to say apples and oranges are the same thing because they're both fruit. They have traits in common, but they aren't the same.

Gold is a good example of money. Currency, on the other hand, is merely a *representation* of money.

So why does this matter? It matters because money grows in value over time, while currencies (meaning *cash* printed by central banks) always lose their value over time.

Here's an example:

The year is 1921, and Mary's wealthy husband gives her $100 and tells her to treat herself to a day of shopping. "Anything you want is fine," he says (providing everything she gets are things he likes and approves of.)

Mary goes to town, and boy oh boy does she ever go to town! After shopping her little bustled-butt off, she comes home with:

- One suit

- One dress
- One skirt
- Two blouses
- One pair of shoes
- One pair of earrings
- And a tube of red lipstick

All for $100. Those were the days, huh?

Now, imagine it's 2021, and Yvonne, who works as an account executive decides to treat herself to a few hours of shopping (no permission required, in this case, because she earned the money herself.)

When Yvonne gets home, she lays her purchases on the bed. They are as follows:

- One suit
- One dress
- One skirt
- Two blouses
- One pair of shoes
- One pair of earrings
- And a tube of red lipstick

The exact same things Mary bought 100-years earlier. Only, when Yvonne gets her credit card statement, the total for the excursion is $1,800.

That is the effect of inflation.

The $100 in currency that bought a bunch of stuff in the past, buys little in the future. Put differently, it takes a lot more cash to buy the same amount of shit today as it did a 100-years ago. You with us so far?

Now, let's change just one thing:

Gold Holds Its Value

Imagine that one hundred years ago, Mary's husband gave her a one-ounce gold coin instead of a hundred dollars in cash. But rather than shopping for clothes, Mary gave the gold coin to her daughter, who handed it down to her daughter, who handed it down to her daughter, who finally said, "Fuck it, I'm going shopping." So, she takes the coin to a coin broker, who gives her $1,800, which she promptly spends it on (you guessed it): the same suit, dress, skirt, blouses, shoes, earrings, and lipstick.

The point? Gold held its value. Currency didn't.

Every time your employer pays you in currency, that currency is like an ice cube that starts melting that very day. The longer you wait to spend it, the less it buys, because prices keep going up.

Ever watched *Pawn Stars*? Great show. Only they get one thing wrong. Rick always tells people he'll pay them in, "cash, money." Sorry, Rick, cash isn't money. If Rick wanted to pay them in real money, he'd have paid them in gold. Or silver. Or platinum. Or plywood. Or pigs. Or chickens. Anything that would hold its value over time.

Recently, at the annual gathering of the world's elite in Davos, Switzerland (attendees included 119 billionaires, 53 heads of state, plus Shakira and Matt Damon), hedge fund manager Ray Dalio told the group, "Cash is trash. Get out of cash." He went on to say that people who got stuck holding cash were going to feel stupid.

No one blinked. They're the global elite, they already knew this was the case.

So where should you put your cash? Well, we know where not to put it, and that's in the stock market.

The stock market isn't a bubble that's going to pop, it's a super-bubble that's going to eventually explode.

So, where do we think you should put your money? Anywhere that isn't in cash, and anywhere that isn't in stocks, that's for sure.

What does that leave?

Well, there's commodities. Like oil. And soybeans. Natural gas. Corn. Wheat. Cattle. Hogs. Lucky Charms. Whatever. And precious metals, of course: gold, silver, platinum, copper, etc.

All these things have a chance at growth, while the experts say cash is certain to drop in value. But do you know what is way better than all of them?

Yeah, you guessed it.

Bitcoin.

"I am in my 20s and seen multiple hyperinflations within my lifetime and had multiple bank accounts being shut down on me. Those experiences sucked big time, but I couldn't be more thankful for it because that's what led me to #Bitcoin."

- @KatietheRussian

Chapter Six

Bitcoin is Digital Gold

While the original idea behind Bitcoin was for it to be a peer-to-peer electronic *cash system*, it is rarely (if ever) used for day-to-day purchases. No one is using Bitcoin to buy a Slurpee from 7-11.

So, it failed, right? No, far from it.

Rather than being adopted as cash ("currency"), Bitcoin has acted more like a precious metal. Specifically, gold. But better than gold. Way better.

As Michael Saylor, CEO of MicroStrategy and one of the world's most knowledgeable Bitcoin supporters, said:

> *"If God created gold in cyberspace, he would have created Bitcoin. It's an encrypted block of sunlight."*

It can't get much better than encrypted sunlight, right? Well, there are still some who prefer gold over Bitcoin, and the debate isn't going to end anytime soon.

Gold vs. Bitcoin: The Great Debate

Here are some things to consider when comparing gold and Bitcoin:

Store of Value

For years, proponents of gold have said there is no better store of value, meaning it holds its value in terms of the U.S. dollar over time. Is this true? Let's look at some numbers.

Over the last 5 years...

- Cash left in your savings account would have paid one percent in interest (if you're lucky)

- An investment in gold would have generated a return of almost 60 percent (which isn't too bad, especially compared to interest on savings)

- But, according to crypto exchange eToro.com, the return on investment (ROI) in Bitcoin was 3,232%

But even with Bitcoin's stunning returns over the last decade, there are still some people who insist gold is the better investment. These people are commonly referred to as *goldbugs*—we call them people who can't let go.

While gold ranks highest in terms of preference for all generations, Bitcoin is the clear choice among Gen Xers and Millennials.

Proven Over Time

Goldbugs love gold (and other precious metals) because they have *proven* themselves over time. *"Gold has been used as money for 4,000 years!"* they scream. *"Why change?"* Yes, gold has value, and it always will. But make no mistake—*Gold is yesterday's money.*

Goldbugs can't seem to accept that the world is changing, and that we're racing toward a digital future.

Let it go, frozen.

Gold is Physical and has "Intrinsic Value"

Goldbugs insist gold is better because it has intrinsic value. It's used to make things, like jewelry and coins. It's also used in computer circuit boards and electroplating. And let's not forget Olympic medals, Oscars® and Grammys®.

Goldbugs also love the fact that you can hold gold in your hand. Ironically, Bitcoiners think Bitcoin is better for the exact opposite reason—because you *can't* hold it in your hand, or at least you don't have to.

Imagine you wanted to move a million dollars of gold from one place to another. What would be involved? $1 million in gold weighs almost eight-hundred pounds. Try putting *that* in the overhead compartment on your next flight.

Conversely, you can carry $100 billion dollars of Bitcoin with you anywhere in the world with a password in your head.

Also, if you own gold, silver, or any precious metal, there are storage issues. Where are you going to keep it, and keep it safe? In a private vault? Safety deposit box at a local bank? Banks have security, sure, but in case of a robbery, safety deposit boxes are not FDIC insured.

Gold Is a "Scarce Commodity"

Another thing goldbugs love to say is that gold is a scarce commodity. Which is true. But there's a big difference between scarce and limited. *Scarce* means it's hard to find, but there's still more out there. *Limited* means there's a hard cap to which something is limited to. So what? Scarce? Limited? To-ma-to, to-mat-o.

Here's why it matters.

At the time we're writing this, gold is selling at $1,750 per ounce. And part of its value is based on the fact that it's expensive to mine and get out of the ground.

Now, suppose the stock market crashes and the dollar collapses in value. Where will all the smart money go? In gold, of course. As a result, the price of gold will skyrocket to $3,000, $5,000, maybe $10,000 per ounce. And when it does, what do you think gold miners will do? They'll start mining like mad, which increases the supply and lowers the price.

You see, gold is scarce, but the supply is not fixed. The more people want it, the more the miners will mine. And get this: insiders say that Elon Musk is planning to mine gold from asteroids in outer space!

Elon has his eye on an asteroid that is believed to have $700 quintillion of gold. To put this in perspective, if the gold on that asteroid was divided equally among the world's population, everyone would be worth $100 billion. Elon Musk wouldn't just be the richest person in the world, he'd be the richest person in the universe. And poverty would be over, right? Nope.

Just like with government printing of cash, the more gold there is, the more prices will inflate. A loaf of bread would cost $30 million, a steak dinner $100 million. And how many asteroids do you think are out there?

Bitcoin Is a "Limited" Commodity

Part of Satoshi Nakamoto's genius is he recognized that for something to maintain its value over time, the supply must be limited. That's why the total number of Bitcoins that will ever be created is capped at 21 million. Period. That's it. There will never be more than 21 million Bitcoins. Ever.

This means that as demand goes up, so will the price—with virtually no upward limit. Some experts predict each Bitcoin will be worth $100,000, others say $500,000 per coin. A few suggest Bitcoin will get to $1 million per coin. There are even a few who believe the price could go as high as $15,000,000 per coin.

And better still, because no more Bitcoin can be "printed," the Federal Reserve can't inflate its value, not to mention that there are no *Bitcoin asteroids* floating in outer space. Sorry, Elon.

(Note: As of February 2021, approximately 18.6 million Bitcoins have been mined. That leaves 2.4 million Bitcoins left to be mined and put into circulation.)

So, which do we think is better, gold or Bitcoin?

Bitcoin, of course.

But don't take our word for it (we aren't financial advisors, remember?) Take the word of Anthony Pompliano, one of the world's most respected Bitcoin experts, who said:

> *"Bitcoin is a 100x improvement over gold as a store of value. I suspect that Bitcoin's market cap will surpass gold's market cap by 2030. For this reason, I own no gold and have a material percent of my net worth invested in Bitcoin."*

Sorry, cash. Sorry, gold and silver.

Sorry soybeans.

"In Bitcoin we trust because in financial freedom we believe. Bitcoin is peaceful protest at its best."

- Maxine Ryan @MaxieRyan

Chapter Seven

The Coming "Wall of Money"

O ne of the most important factors in Bitcoin's rise in value is due to the many institutional investors who are rushing in to buy Bitcoin as a hedge against the rapidly collapsing dollar. Plus, they just like money.

For example, Michael Sonnenshein, the managing director at Grayscale Investments, when being interviewed on CNBC, said, "We are seeing institutional capital flowing in at the fastest pace in the history of our business, and it is being deployed by some of the world's largest institutions and some of the most famous investors."

Because of space limitations, the list of individuals and organizations below represents only a fraction of the big players who have invested in crypto. These are the Whales—investors with enough to move the market when they buy and sell their holdings. But there are thousands of Sharks, Dolphins, Groupers, and Goldfish in the Bitcoin ocean. Us? We're just a couple of Minnows, happier than shit to be swimming with the cool kids in the know.

(Presented in no particular order):

1. Square, Cash App and Twitter

Have you ever seen those square white plastic things retailers use to swipe your credit card? They're from the company Square Inc., a company that helps sellers both large and small to grow their businesses by turning mobile devices into point-of-sale systems.

Jack Dorsey, Square's founder (also the founder of Twitter), is one of Bitcoin's most well-known supporters, and predicted it would one day become the "single currency" of the internet.

As of this writing, Square has purchased 4,709 Bitcoins at around purchase price of $50 million U.S.D. Additionally, Square had over 3 million people transact business in Bitcoin through its Cash App platform in 2020, and the number of users is growing fast.

2. Paul Tudor Jones

American billionaire hedge fund manager, Paul Tudor Jones II, is one of the first big players to invest in Bitcoin, pointing to its potential hedge against inflation. He was quoted saying he believes when the financial history books are written this time will be seen as the seminal moment for the institutional shift towards Bitcoin.

3. MicroStrategy

Michael Saylor, CEO of MicroStrategy, is a strong proponent of Bitcoin and leading the charge to get other companies invested in Bitcoin. He even organized a Bitcoin for Corporations Conference in February 2021. Raoul Pal described a "wall of money" coming into Bitcoin. Saylor added to the sentiment by saying he anticipated an "avalanche of companies" investing at least a portion of their cash into Bitcoin in the next few years.

His message is clearly gaining traction. On New Year's Eve, 2020, investment giant Morgan Stanley revealed that it had purchased 10.9 percent of MicroStrategy. Interesting, huh? Think they know something?

4. Grayscale Bitcoin Trust

One of the biggest names in the Bitcoin space, Grayscale Investments boasts a Bitcoin portfolio of over $30 billion in its Grayscale Bitcoin Trust (which trades under GBTC, should you want to check them out.) They also offer an Ethereum trust and are in the process of planning several others.

5. PayPal

In November 2020, PayPal announced that all its 346 million U.S. account holders could buy, hold, shop and sell Bitcoin (and other selected cryptocurrencies.) Talk about global adoption.

Direct and to the point, PayPal President David A. Marcus summed things up when he said Bitcoin is a "great place to put assets."

6. The City of Miami

While several U.S. municipalities have started showing an interest in Bitcoin, Miami mayor Francis Suarez has put his belief in Bitcoin into action.

In an interview with Forbes, Suarez said he believes Bitcoin will be "the biggest story of the next few years."

With this in mind, Miami may place some of the city's treasury into Bitcoin, and also letting city employees get their salaries *paid* in Bitcoin.

Will other cities follow? Probably. Miami is one hell of a big domino.

7. Tesla

Elon Musk has invested in Bitcoin—$1.5 billion worth, to be precise. Not only did Elon invest in Bitcoin, but he also just announced you can use the cryptocurrency to buy a Tesla.

In January 2021, Musk put #Bitcoin in his Twitter profile, tweeting, "In retrospect, it was inevitable."

8. Blackrock

The world's largest asset manager, Blackrock, with almost $8 trillion assets under management, has filed documents with Securities and Exchange Commission (SEC) to invest in Bitcoin futures. Yep, the biggest financial management firm in the world is now onboard. Blackrock CEO Larry Fink said, "Having a digital currency makes the need for the U.S. dollar to be less relevant." Take that, money printers.

9. Guggenheim Partners

In an interview on CNN, Guggenheim Partners CEO, Scott Minerd, said he believes Bitcoin may eventually climb as high as $600,000 per coin. Guggenheim had looked at Bitcoin for almost 10 years, but the market cap wasn't big enough to invest in—until now. Minerd also said he believed Bitcoin would continue to become more and more important in the global economy.

10. The Winklevoss Twins

Two of the most prominent names in Bitcoin are Cameron and Tyler Winklevoss (aka, "The Winklevoss Twins.") If they sound familiar, it's because they were the two brothers Mark Zuckerberg stole Facebook from in the movie, *The Social Network*. Allegedly.

So how did they get involved? By accident.

On vacation in Ibiza, somebody who recognized them from *The Social Network* asked if they'd thought about Bitcoin, and they hadn't. It sounded kind of crazy to them, but after a shot of tequila, it made more sense.

When they got back to the United States, they started doing some research. Realizing Bitcoin could easily be sent anywhere in the world via the internet, and had the store-of-value properties of gold, they used a chunk of the $65 million they won in the Facebook lawsuit and jumped in. Fast forward nine years, and the twins are multi-billionaires who launched a Bitcoin investment site called Gemini.com. You might say things worked out okay for Cameron and Tyler.

And a Slew of Celebrities

Maybe the only thing that says "cool" more than celebrity endorsements are celebrity investments. Besides Elon Musk and Jack Dorsey, there are some big-name celebrities who have made the leap into crypto, including:

Snoop Dog, Mark Cuban, Kanye West, Hugh Laurie, Floyd Mayweather, Bill Gates, Jamie Foxx, Richard Branson, Ashton Kutcher, and Drew Carey.

Notice anything about this incredible list of leaders, celebrities, and generally smart people? You got it.

They're all guys.

According to one brokerage study released in early 2021, women make up only 15 percent of Bitcoin traders. This must change, bitches, which is why we wrote this book.

The good news is things *are* starting to turn. Crypto buying platforms are reporting that investments by women are skyrocketing by double and triple-digit percentages.

In 2020, Investopedia profiled five of the world's top Bitcoin millionaires and one of them was (drumroll) a woman: Blythe Masters. A former Managing Director at J.P. Morgan Chase & Co., today she's CEO of Digital Asset Holdings, a company that builds "encryption-based processing tools to improve the efficiency, security, and compliance of securities trading—specifically Bitcoin." (Um, yeah, she's just a little impressive.)

And just as we were editing this manuscript, Paris Hilton was asked if she was invested in Bitcoin and she said, "Yes, I'm very, very excited about it, it's definitely the future."

Bitcoin as an investment was once thought of as a contrarian idea. It is fast becoming a *consensus* position.

And if you don't think being invested Bitcoin is a good idea after reading this section, there's nothing more we can do to help. As the saying goes, we can *explain* Bitcoin to you, but we can't *understand* it for you.

"My family went from mocking me to envying me. Feels kinda good. Thanks #Bitcoin."

- Py Patel @PieceofthePy

Chapter Eight

Arguments Against Bitcoin

Yes, we are true believers when it comes to Bitcoin, but we would be remiss if we didn't share some of the arguments against it. Some of the arguments are valid concerns. Most of them are nonsensical bullshit. In any case, they deserve to be addressed.

Bitcoin is Extremely Volatile

The dictionary definition of *volatile* is *"a statistical measure of dispersion of returns, measured by using the standard deviation or variance between returns from that same security or market index."* WTF? Talk about word salad.

Having been involved in crypto for a bit, our definition is more realistic. *"Holy, fuck, Bitcoin dropped 12 percent overnight!"*

Detractors love to point out just how volatile Bitcoin can be—and they love the word *bubble*. Some can't say it enough.

- At least eight Nobel Prize winners have described Bitcoin as a *bubble*. Famous billionaire investor Warren Buffet called Bitcoin a *mirage*.

- New York University professor Nouriel Roubini one-upped Buffet by calling Bitcoin the *"mother of all bubbles."* A simple bubble wasn't enough.

- Economist Paul Krugman said Bitcoin was *"a bubble wrapped in techno-mysticism inside a cocoon of libertarian ideology"* (whatever in the fuck that means.)

If you're going to get involved in Bitcoin, you better get used to it. Volatility comes with the territory. For example, look at the price chart for Bitcoin:

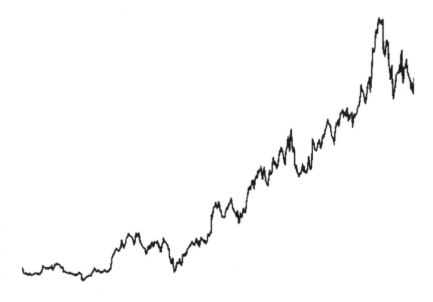

Oh, sorry, wrong chart. This is Amazon.

Ah, here we go...

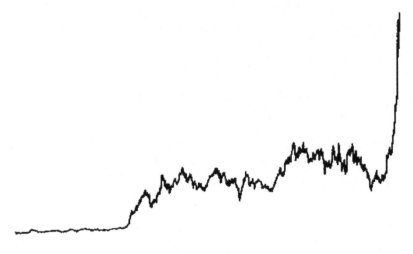

Oops, screwed up again. This is Tesla.

Okay, one more try:

Yes, finally—this is Bitcoin's chart.

Now, look at all three charts and what do they have in common? The answer is: Volatility.

Things that grow in value over time experience volatility.

Most people think of volatility as something to avoid, something undesirable. But what if the exact opposite were true? What if volatility was what we wanted? Well, it is. Volatility is good.

Want proof? Okay, look at this chart:

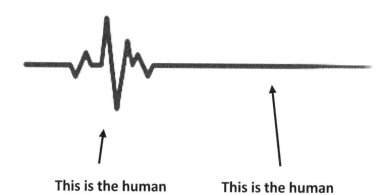

This is the human heart when volatile.   **This is the human heart when it's not.**

Take your pick.

Things that are alive are volatile.

Get over it.

Bitcoin is a Ponzi Scheme

Is Bitcoin a Ponzi scheme? In a word, no. In two words: Fuck, no.

Named after early-1900s fraudster Charles Ponzi, Ponzi schemes:

- Guarantee a high rate of return with little or no risk. This is not the case with Bitcoin.

- Promise a consistent flow of returns regardless of what's happening in the marketplace. Again, this does not describe Bitcoin. If anything, Bitcoin is often like being on a highly volatile rollercoaster.

- Are presented as "secret strategies" which the organizer refuses to share with investors. Bitcoin is the opposite—it's open-source for all to see.

- Investors usually have long waiting periods for removing their money (read: time needed by the organizer to get new money from some other sucker.) Bitcoin, on the other hand, is sold on open exchanges that allow investors to sell/cash out anytime they want.

People think anything that requires new people to come in at the bottom so the people at the top can make money off them are Ponzi schemes. If this is your definition, then you've just described every company in the world that needs new entry-level workers to work long hours for less money than the people at the top. For example: law firms that require recent law school graduates to slave away eighty-to-one-hundred hours per week to have a chance at making partner.

So, let's put this Ponzi scheme/scam thing to bed, shall we? Bitcoin is nothing like a Ponzi scheme. It's open source, transparent, verifiable, and auditable. Only people who remain willfully ignorant on the subject continue to use the "p" word.

Bitcoin is Used by Drug Dealers

Admittedly, Bitcoin had a rough start in terms of public perception since the first major users were black markets—specifically, the Silk Road.

Lunched in February 2021, the Silk Road was a "dark web" website. It was basically a marketplace for a lot of illegal shit. During the thirty months it operated, it accepted only Bitcoin as payment. Because of this, a narrative emerged suggesting Bitcoin was something bad used by drug smugglers, and other nefarious actors.

Later that year, the FBI seized ₿30,000 from the Silk Road following the arrest of its founder and operator, Ross Ulbricht. The seized Bitcoin were sold off in a blind, on-line auction by the U.S. Marshal Service.

The buyer was well-known Silicon Valley investor Tim Draper. Draper concluded the government felt the currency was legal—if not, why would they be selling it?

The truth is, money can be used for good and evil, and the argument that Bitcoin must be stopped because a few people have used it, or will use it, for unlawful activity makes it bad? If that is your criteria, we better make cash illegal. We hear drug dealers use that cash shit all the time.

Governments Will Ban Bitcoin!

No, they won't. Governments will tax the living fuck out of it because that's what governments do. But ban it? No. They'll whine and threaten and saber-rattle, but if they try to ban it, they will fail. Bitcoin is the future, and the future is unbannable. The future is coming, and Bitcoin will be part of it.

Bitcoin Uses a Lot of Electricity

Bitcoin is often criticized for the amount of electricity that is consumed through the process of Bitcoin mining. People who say this fail to recognize the enormous energy used to by our *existing* banking system. If you want to get down in the mud about terawatts, don't forget to include the amount of energy used by bank computers, bank branches, the banks themselves (keeping the heat and lights on), not to mention the amount of energy central banks use to print, store and distribute cash. Oh, and how much energy do you think is used to operate the 3.2 million ATMs around the world?

According to Politico, Bitcoin's total energy consumption is only about 6 percent of the total power consumed by the global banking sector.

People who complain about Bitcoin's energy consumption have good intentions, but they don't have all the facts. And if the complaint about energy use is out of concern for the planet, consider the fact that the crypto mining industry goes out of its way to use renewable energy sources.

Satoshi Nakamoto's amazing invention is far more energy-efficient than people think.

Hackers Might Steal Your Bitcoin

Finally, something to be concerned over.

Bitcoins that are held at exchanges are vulnerable to theft by hackers. Not as much today as during the early years of cryptocurrency, but some risk always exists. Hackers, hack. It's what they do. Protecting your Bitcoin is important. We'll talk a little more about this in a bit.

You Don't "Get It"

Finally, one of the biggest things that holds people back from investing in Bitcoin is the inability to wrap their brain around what blockchain technology is and how it works. We barely get it ourselves.

The funny thing is people have no problem investing in Amazon stock. Why? They think they understand Amazon because they shop on Amazon.com, place an order, their credit card gets charged and the product shows up on their porch. So, they're willing to invest.

But do they really understand what they're investing in? Do they really understand the fundamentals of Amazon's business operations? For example, what is Amazon's current cash flow projections? Return on assets? Who are the five key players on their management team? How do the conveyer belts work? How products are received, stocked, and shipped to distribution centers for delivery? Are there any lawsuits pending? Do they understand *any* of this? No. People invest in Amazon *thinking* they understand, but the truth is they don't know shit. But that's okay.

Here's a question: What do you really understand about gravity? Or electricity? Or the mathematical formulas behind Einstein's theory of space-time?

The answer is: *nothing.*

All you know is that if you jump off a cliff, you're going down, not up. And if you flip the wall switch, the lights go on. And as far as Einstein goes, fuck it—there are only a dozen people or so who understanding any of his theories.

Bottom line?

All you really need to understand to invest in Bitcoin is this:

1. There are a lot of very smart people who do understand it and are personally invested in it.

2. Traditional banking systems are flawed, and Bitcoin will be the main currency in the future.

3. Governments think their citizens (aka, all of us) are cattle, grazing in a field, waiting to be financially slaughtered when it suits them.

And which cows will escape the slaughter? Only the cows with wings made of Bitcoin.

"Make money and build something for yourself because I assure you no one is coming to save you."

- Layah Heilpern @LayahHeilpern

Section Three:

Resources for Buying, Storing & Learning More About Cryptocurrencies

Chapter Nine

Altcoins vs. "Shitcoins"

Before we get into buying, storing and selling cryptocurrencies, we need to take a moment to talk about "Altcoins."

So far, this book has been Bitcoin-focused for a good reason: we believe Bitcoin is the only coin you really need to invest in to make money and protect yourself from inflation. The main reason is Bitcoin's size (and trust us here: *size does matter.*)

The total cryptocurrency market just reached a market cap of $2 trillion. Almost 60 percent of that is in Bitcoin; the 9,000+ other cryptocurrencies share the other 40 percent. That's how big and far ahead Bitcoin is.

Bitcoin is Godzilla.

Altcoins are Chihuahuas nipping at Bitcoin's ankles.

As a rule, companies with the biggest market cap in any industry represent the lowest risk. Apple, Microsoft, Facebook, and Google are good examples.

But this is not to say there aren't other cryptocurrencies you may want to invest in. There are. We're invested in some Altcoins ourselves, but we didn't start there. We started with Bitcoin. To not even mention them would be wrong.

What is an Altcoin?

By definition, an Altcoin is any cryptocurrency that isn't Bitcoin. They are *alternatives* to Bitcoin. And because Bitcoin was the first successful crypto, every Altcoin in existence was created after Bitcoin.

While the total market value of Altcoins is nowhere near that of Bitcoin's, some have been growing at an even faster rate. Ethereum and Cardano are two good examples—we own some of each.

The truth is most of the Altcoin projects that get launched will never make money for their investors, assuming they materialize into anything at all. This means they are incredibly risky investments. You may be better off going to Vegas (let us know, we'll join you, but not to gamble, just for drinks.)

The things we consider when investing in any Altcoin come down to:

- Do we understand what its designed to do?
- Who has money invested in it?
- How many of the experts are excited about it and recommending it?
- Lastly, do we have a few extra bucks that we can afford to lose if things go badly?

The Big Altcoins Today

The top ten Cryptocurrencies with their current market capitalizations as of April 2021:

1. Bitcoin $1.1 trillion
2. Ethereum $ 250 billion

3.	Binance Coin	$ 60 billion
4.	Ripple XRP	$ 50 billion
5.	Tether	$ 43 billion
6.	Polkadot	$ 42 billion
7.	Cardano	$ 40 billion
8.	Uniswap	$ 16 billion
9.	Litecoin	$ 15 billion
10.	Chainlink	$ 14 billion

As a frame of reference, the $25,000^{th}$ crypto on the list is *HorusPay*, with a market capitalization of $307, 675.

What Problem Does the Coin Solve?

The majority of cryptocurrencies are Bitcoin-wannabes. Only a few are actually working to solve a problem and fill a true need in the new digital marketplace.

Figuring out why a certain crypto coin was created and what its mission is, will take the greatest amount of time on your part. It will also be the most rewarding. There's nothing like the feeling when a particular crypto project makes sense to you, you invest, and then months later, you watch it begin to blossom and grow.

For example, we heard about a crypto currency called EOS. We looked it up on Kraken.com and checked out the description which said:

> *EOS is built for a variety of use cases from social media to health care and makes it easy for developers to create decentralized applications (dapps) as it uses programming languages that are popular outside of blockchain technology.*

Does this tell us everything there is to know about EOS? No. But *social media* and *healthcare* piqued our interest. After a bit more digging, we decided to buy some EOS. A month later it had gone up 66 percent. Admittedly, it could have gone up or down. In either case, at least we'd have made an informed decision.

Again, if your investment strategy goes beyond just Bitcoin, there is a lot to learn, like:

- Defi
- Dapps
- NFTs
- Stablecoins
- Gold-backed coins

And more. One place to check out is:

https://coinmarketcap.com/alexandria/glossary

Here you'll find a glossary of good-to-know terms. It will take you an hour or two to read through all of them. It may seem daunting to wrap your brain around all this information, but if you don't have at least a few hours to study this stuff, then don't invest in altcoins.

Altcoins vs. "Shitcoins"

As you get involved in the world of cryptocurrencies, you may hear the term "shitcoins." To some people, any coin that isn't Bitcoin is a "shitcoin."

We disagree.

Sure, there is a new coin launched every day, and many of them are indeed, shit. They'll never be worth anything. And some cryptos are out-and-out scams, designed for no other purpose than to get you to invest so they can run off to some island with your hard-earned money. Shame on those fuckers. But this does not mean *all* Altcoins are shit. Far from it. Many are great investments, some maybe better than Bitcoin. The top ten coins we listed previously fit this category.

If you'd like to invest in things other than just Bitcoin, do your research, bitches, and learn about the various cryptocurrencies. How are they different? What is their purpose? What need do they serve in the marketplace? We could tell you, but that would be like giving you a fish. Our mission is not to feed you for a day, it's to get you catching your own damn fish.

We avoid being swayed by one Facebook post, one tweet, one YouTube video, one Clubhouse conversation, one telegram mention, or one friend's recommendation at the watercooler. Investing your hard-earned cash relying on *one* piece of information is dumb, including trusting information in just this one book. Read. Watch. Google. Ask. Listen.

Oh, yeah, and think.

The more information you get, the more confident you'll be in your decision. And even if it turns out to be a dud, at least you won't find yourself saying, "Why did I invest in that?" You'll know why you did, and that goes a long way to avoiding kicking yourself in the ass with regret.

Experts You Should Follow

If you're going to attempt investing in anything other than the four to five highest market cap cryptocurrencies, you should learn more from the serious experts in the space. For our money (literally, *for our money*), the experts *we* follow most (in no particular order) include:

1. Anthony Pompliano (aka, Pomp)

2. Max Keiser & Stacy Herbert (Orange Pill podcast and Keiser Report)

3. Cathie Wood (CEO of ARK Investments)

4. Andres Antonopoulos

5. Aaron Arnold (Altcoin Daily)

6. Danielle DiMartino Booth

7. Lyn Alden

8. Casey Leigh Henry (Crypto Casey)

9. Raoul Pal (Real Vision)

10. Willie Woo

11. Caitlin Long

12. Simon Dixon (Bank to the Future)

13. Dan Held (of Kraken)

14. Robert Breedlove

15. Michael Saylor (CEO, MicroStrategy)

There are many others of course, but this is a damned good start. These people are on all the social platforms including

YouTube, Twitter, and are either hosts or frequent guests on podcasts.

Also, please don't forget to follow the fabulous women crypto experts we've quoted throughout this book. This should be the beginning of your crypto education bitches, not the end!

Special warning: Another fucking warning? A small one, but important. Keep in mind when you are on social media (Twitter, IG, etc.) sometimes you'll see people shilling particular coins because they are being paid by the owners of the project. The only way to get the right information is by listening to people who have earned your trust over time.

Also, there are a shit-ton of outright scams. Impersonations are big: People pretending to be a well-known crypto expert giving away Bitcoin. All they need for you to do is send them a little of your Bitcoin first. Obviously, these people are not sitting around trying to send you free crypto. They're nice, but not *that* nice.

Because this is the new Wild West, there are a lot of bad guys out there taking advantage of newbie investors. It shouldn't need to be said but we will anyway. Never, ever, give anyone your username or password for any account. Always do your research, bitches!

"Goldman, J.P. Morgan, Morgan Stanley, and others will offer Bitcoin only to their wealthy clients. You don't need someone in a suit to tell you about Bitcoin. Bitcoin is for everyone."

- Meltem Demirors @Melt_Dem

Chapter Ten

Buying and Storing Bitcoin

This could easily be the most complicated section of the book, but we refuse to do that to you. Instead, we're going to only cover what you *must* know to get started and keep even that simple. If you want to dive into tons of advanced shit, just Google "I'm bored, please teach me stuff I don't need to know about Bitcoin."

That said, let's start with the obvious...

Where to Buy Bitcoin

The good news is it has never been easier to buy and sell cryptocurrencies. This was not always the case. Yes, there are a few hoops to jump through, but compared to five years ago, buying Bitcoin is a piece of cake.

By the way, now is also a good time to make something clear in case you are confused: you do *not* have to buy an *entire* Bitcoin! (Or any other cryptocurrency for that matter.) You can choose to buy fifty dollars of Bitcoin, or five-thousand dollars of Bitcoin. The platform you buy on will then calculate what percentage of a Bitcoin you own. So, when we talk about "coins" you may not own a full Bitcoin for a while, but that doesn't matter.

The simplest way to buy is through an online crypto exchange. To see a list of the Top 100 Exchanges (yes, there are hundreds) we recommend going to coingecko.com. Not only does CoinGecko offer a comprehensive list of exchanges, but it also rates them in terms of trust by providing a "trust score."

We have not researched every one of these exchanges, and we are not making recommendations. All we can tell you is it's probably best to stick with bigger exchanges that have a proven track record with the public (hence the importance of the trust scores.)

The exchanges **_we_** have used include:

- Coinbase

- Robinhood

- Swan Bitcoin

- Gemini

- Kraken

- Bittrex

There are many other exchanges. For example, Binance is the world's largest exchange by trading volume. It's probably great as are many others. The six listed above are the ones _we_ happen to have experience with.

You may be wondering: _Why use multiple exchanges?_ Was there some kind of problem that made us keep switching? No. We've never had a problem with any of the exchanges we've used, and have coins stored at most of them to this day.

The reason we use multiple exchanges is because we're a couple of paranoid bitches who don't want to keep all our eggs in one basket. You know, just in case.

In case of what? Who the fuck knows? In the same way people open multiple accounts at different banks, having your crypto in multiple locations seemed like a good idea, should there be an issue with one exchange. It only makes sense.

Factors When Choosing an Exchange

As you can imagine, every exchange will tell you they're the best and sell you on why you should use them over the others. Duh, it's called marketing. But there are a few things you want to review closely, the most important of which are:

- What are the fees for buying crypto through their exchange?

- Can you transfer the crypto into your own wallet, or do you have to keep your crypto stored on their exchange?

- Do they have a good safety history?

- What is the process for getting your money if you want to sell? How long does it take? Is there a withdrawal fee involved?

- Is your money insured?

Let's start with fees.

Fees

Fees are how the exchanges make money—without them, they go out of business. There's no way to escape paying at least some fees. But this does not mean you have to pay *bitchrageous* fees.

Different exchanges charge varying fees for different activities: wire transfer fees, fees for buying, fees for selling, fees for withdrawing your money. So, it's a good idea to read the fine print. This goes for any kind of investment.

For example:

- Trading fees at Kraken range from 0.16 percent to 0.26 percent, and there's no fee for withdrawing your money from the exchange.

- At Bittrex, the trading fee is 0.35 percent (which is higher) and there is also fee for fund withdrawal.

So, why would anyone choose Bittrex over Kraken? Well, we signed up for Bittrex to invest in a crypto coin called Library (LBRY), and at that time, they were the only exchange that offered it, so the fees were not the main factor.

To get the latest on the different fees being charged by different exchanges, here are a couple websites to get information:

- Cointracker.io
- Bitcoinprice.com

Because the world of cryptocurrency is moving so fast, it's hard to keep up with fees, so no matter when you're reading this, anything we say here may be outdated. These are strictly examples. DYORB!

Where to Store Your Crypto

Once you buy the Bitcoin, you have to decide where to keep it.

The two ways to "custody" your Bitcoin are:

1. Controlling it yourself *(aka, self-custody)*

2. Trusting someone else to do it for you *(aka, leaving it where you bought it.)*

If you decide to take custody of your coins, you'll be 100% responsible for your coins.

The good news is you get to be in total control. The bad news is you assume the responsibility to be in total control.

In the end, the questions you'll need to answer are:

- Who do I trust more, myself or the exchange?
- Do I want the responsibility and the hassle of holding my own coins?

One of the mantras you'll hear a lot is:

Not your keys, not your coins.

What it means is that if you don't have your coins in your possession, they are subject to hackers or government confiscation.

Are we telling you there is a high likelihood of having your account hacked if you keep your coins on an exchange? No. The likelihood is very low. Extremely low, actually. And the likelihood of the government telling the exchanges to turn all the crypto in their possession over to them because they're stupid broke fuckers is very low, also. But, anything is possible. Never underestimate the cleverness of hackers or the stupidity of our leaders.

Cold vs. Hot Wallet

When you buy your crypto on an exchange—like some of those we listed, it's known as a "hot wallet" and it basically means it's accessible online and connected to the internet. A "cold wallet" on the other hand is not connected to the web and is usually a piece of hardware where you can "store" your coins. You can order these online and they look like USB drives. (The two most popular now are called Trezor and Ledger.) It's the next level of security for your digital assets but you must be very careful with these.

You may have at some point heard some horror story that someone "lost" millions of dollars in Bitcoin? (There have been dozens of these, and they are all true.) It's typically because the person either lost the physical device or they forgot the highly complex security phrase that's required to access it. And guess what? There's no customer service and no one to call. You are customer service.

We mention the cold wallet option because at some point you should investigate it. Many people store some crypto online and have more in a cold wallet.

Self-Custody is Best, Right?

Not necessarily.

With self-custody *you* are responsible for storing and protecting your coins. This means transferring your coins to a digital wallet, which has to be done extremely carefully because if you make a mistake on the address—even one wrong character—your coins will be lost. Like in unretrievable. Forever.

Seriously.

Next, since you are storing your own digital assets, what happens if there is a break-in? The safest place to keep your assets is in a safe, of course. So, you'll need to buy one—a big heavy safe that can't be easily carried off—and, ideally, the safe should be bolted to the floor.

Don't want to have a home safe? You could put your crypto wallet in a safety deposit box at a bank, but now you're trusting a bank to keep it safe. Shit, if you're going to put your trust in a third party, why not just trust the exchange you bought them from?

See how complicated this is already getting?

To be clear, we are <u>not</u> trying to scare you out of investing in Bitcoin. We're just pointing this out, so you know what in the fuck people are talking about when you hear this.

"Imagine not buying #Bitcoin for your family's future, especially your children!"

- @CryptoWendyO

Chapter Eleven
Be a HODLer, Not a Trader

I f you get involved in the Bitcoin scene, you're sure to encounter people who will tell you to "hodl." No, this is not a typo (although this *is* how the term got its start.)

The term hodl first appeared in a blog post in 2013 titled, "I AM HODLING." He meant to say he was *holding*. Since that time, the term hodl has become part of common language within the Bitcoin community.

The concept of *hodling* is not just the adoption of a simple misspelled word, it represents an ideology that encourages people not to sell their Bitcoin. Since then, H.O.D.L. is often used as an acronym which stands for *Hold On for Dear Life*.

So, why is it important to *hodl?*

Because Bitcoin is volatile. Sometimes it feels like riding a bucking bronco. Sadly, people who panic when Bitcoin goes down often make the decision sell, only to watch it soar in price afterward. Holding on guarantees eventual profit—assuming one doesn't sell too soon. People who hold and don't sell always do well. Those who give into F.U.D. (Fear, Uncertainty and Doubt) don't.

The best part about hodling is it eliminates the need to become a trading expert. All you need to do is buy, *and then do fucking nothing.* Just sit back and let time take care of everything.

HODLing is Smart

Here's a review of Bitcoin's growth and volatility:

- **2009:** Bitcoins were first issued. Value? $0.00.

- **2010:** Bitcoin is offered for sale with a starting bid of $50. Only a few were sold. The year ended with Bitcoin at $0.39. (Note: On May 22 of that year, 10,000 Bitcoin were used to buy two pizzas.)

- **2011:** Bitcoin reaches $1, then a surge takes it to approximately $31. Soon afterward, it crashes back down to $2.

- **2012:** Bitcoin's value rises to approximately $13.

- **2013:** A financial crisis in Cyprus sends Bitcoin's price soaring. The end of the year finds it at $750.

- **2014:** A bad, bad year for Bitcoin. Bitcoin's largest exchange, Mt. Gox, went bankrupt, and rumors about a Bitcoin ban in China start to swirl. Bitcoin's value goes down to $300.

- **2015:** Bitcoin enters a bull market with a value of over $400, then dips to $150. The number of companies accepting Bitcoin grows and Barclays Bank becomes the first bank to accept Bitcoin investments, sending the value to $360.

- **2016:** Bitcoin is recognized as a currency in Japan and its value rises to almost $1,000.

- **2017:** Holy fuck! Bitcoin soars to just under $20,000!

- **2018:** WTF? Bitcoin drops like a rock and ends the year at $3,500.

- **2019:** Bitcoin starts the year in a slump, trading in the $3,900-$4,000 range. But in April, Bitcoin starts to climb and goes all the way to $13,000 per coin but ends the year near $7,300 per coin.

- **2020:** Covid-19 arrives and takes the wind out of Bitcoin's sails and sends it crashing down to $5,000. By October, BTC climbs to $10,000. By Christmas, BTC is over $26,000, a new all-time high (ATH.)

- **2021:** Bitcoin soars to $30,000. Then $40,000. Then $50,000. Then it hits $60,000. At the time we're writing this, Bitcoin is bouncing between $55,000-$59,000.

Just in case you missed the point: Anyone and everyone who bought Bitcoin anywhere along the way and held it, has made money.

The only people who got screwed on Bitcoin were people who bought it, then panicked when the price went down and sold it at a loss.

But it's Too Late Now

Now, you may be thinking, "That's great for everyone else, but at $50,000, it's too late now." Wake the fuck up, bitches. It's not too late, it's still early.

Here are the current predictions* as to where the price of Bitcoin will go:

- J.P. Morgan says Bitcoin could climb to $130,000.

- CoinCorner crypto exchange CEO, Danny Scott, forecast that Bitcoin would climb as high as $83,000 by the end of April 2021.

- Former hedge fund manager, James Altucher, predicted a $1 million Bitcoin price.

- Plan B's "stock-to-flow" model (one of the most reliable predictors thus far) predicts a 2021 Bitcoin price of $100,000 to $288,000, and $1 million by 2026.

- Early adopter and Bitcoin Evangelist, Max Keiser, predicts $230,000 by the end of 2021.

- Wave Financial issued a report that suggests Bitcoin will reach $400,000 by 2025.

- Bloomberg predicts a $400,000 Bitcoin price in 2021.

- Pantera Capital predicts Bitcoin will climb as high as $115,000 by summer 2021.

- Analyst Peter Brandt sees Bitcoin going somewhere between $180,000 to $200,000 by the end of 2021.

- BTIG set a Bitcoin price prediction of $95,000 by the end of 2022.

- Michael Saylor, CEO of MicroStrategy (who owns more than 90,000 Bitcoin) says Bitcoin has the potential to reach a market cap of $100 trillion. If that happens, a single Bitcoin will be $5 million.

*These are only predictions. Obviously, there's no guarantee.

So, what will Bitcoin *actually* go to? How the fuck should we know? Do we look like Nostradamus? But if the best predictor of *future* performance is *past* performance, why isn't $100,000 possible? Or $250,000. Or $500,000?

Or $1 million.

From its price of $100 in 2013, Bitcoin is up 600X. If it were to go up another 100X from where it is today, that would take Bitcoin to $6 million per coin.

And you're thinking it's too late?

2013: It's too late to buy Bitcoin.

2014: It's too late to buy Bitcoin.

2015: It's too late to buy Bitcoin.

2016: It's too late to buy Bitcoin.

2017: It's too late to buy Bitcoin.

2018: It's too late to buy Bitcoin.

2019: It's too late to buy Bitcoin.

2020: It's too late to buy Bitcoin.

"I don't know who needs to see this, but you haven't missed out on Bitcoin. This is still the early stage."

- Bella Farina @BitcoinBF (March 2021)

Chapter Twelve

No One is Coming to Save You

Did this book cover everything you needed to understand Bitcoin and other cryptocurrencies? Fuck no. We'd have needed 10,000 pages and a lot of nerd-worthy text to even get close. But hopefully we did achieve three things:

1. Convinced you the economy is in shambles, the stock market is crashing, inflation is coming, and "the man" (in the form of the government and the Federal Reserve) do *not* have your back.

2. Made you aware of Bitcoin and how it might well be a life raft for millions of people when the shit hits the proverbial fan.

3. Provided you with enough reasons to pull out your checkbook and buy some before it's too late.

When digital cryptocurrencies arrived, it sounded like something out of a sci-fi novel. And most women aren't all that into science-fiction. They also tend to be more risk-averse than their male counterparts, which is perhaps why they've been standing on the sidelines during this once in a century financial opportunity. That needs to end.

Fortunately, studies have shown the gender landscape is changing. Grayscale, who operates the Grayscale Bitcoin Trust, says account openings by female investors is skyrocketing, while other studies show women now comprising between 40-45 percent of all Bitcoin investors. That number is up almost 15 percent from last year. We'd love to see that number double.

Building Wealth Is a Marathon, Not a Sprint

We've mentioned Michael Saylor several times in this book and with good reason: he's rich, he's smart, and remember the yacht featured in the TV series *Entourage?* That's his. Oh, and the man has over $2 billion of his own money invested in Bitcoin.

Guys like Michael Saylor don't make investments that might cause them to lose their yacht—they make investments that will let them buy more yachts. So, when Michael Saylor speaks, we listen. On a recent YouTube video, he pointed out the following facts:

- Bitcoin is a trillion-dollar digital monetary network, the most successful thing you've ever seen in your life. Period.

- It took Microsoft 44 years to be a trillion-dollar network.

- It took Apple 42 years to be a trillion-dollar network.

- It took Amazon 24 years to be a trillion-dollar network.

- It took Google 22 years to be a trillion-dollar network.

- It only took Bitcoin 12 years to become a trillion-dollar network.

Do we have your attention, bitches?

Bitcoin, though rising at a meteoric pace, is still not moving fast enough for some people. We live in a give-me-mine-now world, where everyone expects to get rich overnight. Bitcoin may be the closest thing to it in the history of the world. And all we have to do is buy and bide our time.

Which brings us to something that bugs the living shit out of us.

When Lambo

"When Lambo?" is crypto-slang for, *"When is Bitcoin going to make me rich enough to buy my Lamborghini?"* This is the kind of bullshit most often heard from the mouths of young millennial men who lack the patience and maturity to think more than six inches from their groins. No, make that four inches.

Having a *When Lambo* mindset is destructive.

Here's why:

Imagine you had enough money to buy an entire Bitcoin, which would be approximately $60,000 today. Now, how much is a Lambo?

The cheapest Lamborghini model is the Urus, with a sticker price around $210,000. It's the low end, but good enough for our example.

So, let's say Bitcoin goes up 500 percent, turning your $60k into $300k. After tax, you've got enough to buy it!

So, you sell your Bitcoin, buy your car, and life is perfect. Well, almost perfect. You still live in a house with an unpaid mortgage (or worse, paying rent in an apartment) and you're still stuck in your job and you're no closer to being free. But at least you've got a Lambo—a Lambo you can barely afford to pay the insurance on.

Five years passes and you know what happens? Bitcoin goes to $1 million, and you realize you could have had the Lambo, put $100k down on a house in a gated community, and maybe even quit your job.

How's the Lambo looking now? It looks stupid.

The answer to *When Lambo?* is ten years from now, because in ten years a single Bitcoin may be worth $10 million. And if that happens, you don't need a Lambo to impress strangers because you've got something 10X better. You've got freedom.

Fuck this *"When Lambo?"* shit. The question you should be asking is, "When freedom?" Freedom, bitches, that's what this Bitcoin thing is all about.

Fairy Tales Aren't Free

Most young girls have dreams of living a fairy tale life. We know we did. (Branden even wrote a fabulous book about it!) The problem with the dream is we expect that fairy tale life to be handed to us. As we get older, we figure out that's bullshit; even if we *do* get the fairy tale life, we've got to work our Cinderella-asses off for it.

Maybe you can relate.

One of the most terror-filled moments for most of us is the realization that no one is coming to save us.

No one.

It's easy to blame others because things didn't work out the way we thought they would. It's the world's fault. And the government's fault. And rich people's fault. And... and... and...

The truth is, where we find ourselves at any given moment in time is our fault; at a minimum it's our *responsibility*.

The fairy tale is possible. We can be saved. But if you want to have the life of your dreams, you're going to have to save yourself. Bitcoin is the tool to do exactly that.

If you want Bitcoin to go to work for you, you're going to have to buy some Bitcoin. Which brings us to the topic of how much you can afford to invest.

For some people, the answer to this is $500. For others it may be $1,000, $5,000 or more. For others it's nothing.

If you think you have nothing to invest, you need to get your head out of your ass. You *do* have money to invest—at least you could if you wanted to. The problem is that you're spending money on needless bullshit. For example:

- Go out to dinner lately? What did it cost? $75? $100. More?

- Go out for drinks lately? How much did you drop at the bar? $20? $30? $50?

- Buy any new clothing lately, something you wanted but really didn't need? Don't lie, bitches, you know it's true. Dress: $80. Blouse: $65.

- Now let's talk shoes. $100. $150. $250?

- Rings? Earrings? Bracelets? Should we continue?

We know what you're thinking. You're thinking, *"But, you don't understand. If I can't go out and buy new clothes, what's the point of working my ass off?"*

Okay, let us help you here. The point of working your ass off shouldn't be escapism—it should be freedom. Freedom, bitches. No clothing looks as good as freedom feels. No alcohol tastes as good as telling your asshole boss, "Guess what? I quit." And freedom requires sacrifice.

Fact: You can't have the life you want without giving up the life you've got. You can't get thin eating fattening shit. You can't run a marathon without getting your ass off the sofa to train. And you can't have a life of freedom spending every penny you make on bullshit when you could be investing it in something that can make you free.

Decide to Change Your Life

Starting right now, this very minute, make the decision to change your life by stopping spending money on anything that you absolutely do not need, which if you're honest, is a lot more than you're probably willing to admit.

And here's something that should send shivers down your spine: That $65 blouse isn't really a $65 blouse—it's a $6,500 blouse. How? Because that's what that same $65 is probably going to be worth in ten years. That $150 dinner? $15,000. It had better have been one hell of a great bottle of wine and filet mignon for that price.

Shoes and jewelry are not the only way to happiness. For that matter, screw happiness—go for joy, instead.

- *Joy is wealth.*
- *Joy is freedom.*
- *Joy is dying without regrets.*

For years we rolled our eyes at the whole *"pay yourself first"* mantra. You know, the idea that you need to put 10 percent of your paycheck in savings before you pay all your bills.

Then you tithe 10 percent to the church.

Ideally you invest the next 10 percent in personal development. Whatever is left is what you're supposed to live off.

We don't know a single fucking person who does this. Maybe they're out there, but we've never met them. That kind of discipline is way beyond our pay grade. This said, it *is* a good idea to get in the habit of paying yourself first, in this case for the purposes of investing in Bitcoin. It takes discipline, but it's worth it.

One great way we know of doing this is the automatic investment program at SwanBitcoin.com. You sign up, tell them how much you want to deduct from your account each week, and forget about it. If you need to pause the deductions, you can, with the push of a button.

Your Future is Calling

If you want the future of your dreams, you've got to be willing to sacrifice and suffer at least a little bit. You must be willing to postpone luxury, comfort, and immediate gratification for something bigger and better somewhere on down the road.

Are you willing to do that?

Are you willing to say "no" to some of the things you want, to have the money to invest in Bitcoin?

We'll tell you this: If the answer is "no," we predict that five years from now your life will be almost exactly like it is right now. In fact, it will be worse. Because five years from now you're going to look back at this moment—right now, reading this book—and realize you had your chance.

The good news is, it's not five years from now. It's now.

You still have your chance.

May We Ask for a Favor?

If you've enjoyed this book, we ask you to please share what you learned with other women who need it. Give it as a gift to others. Buy a copy for your mom. And your aunt. Your sister. Your friends. Your sister's friends.

There's a saying that, as women, we must *straighten each other's crowns*. Well, if we teach another woman about Bitcoin, she can buy whatever the hell kind of crown she damn well pleases!

Wait, did we say *one* favor?

Also, would you also be so kind as to write a review on Amazon? If you'd pop over and drop us a quick review it would mean the world to us!

That's it.

Now, go buy some Bitcoin, bitches!

About Branden LaNette...

BRANDEN doesn't look like a typical author, but she has long ignored what she "should" do, say and look like. On her own at a young age, Branden managed to find herself with the wrong guy, the wrong job, and a bleak future.

Step by step, decision by decision, Branden learned to turn heartbreak into happiness <u>and</u> self-judgment into inner joy.

Today, Branden is an entrepreneur, coach, speaker, wife, mom, and bestselling author.

Her first book, *Once Upon a Time, Bitches,* was published in 2019. This book is her fourth, with a fifth coming in October 2021. Her goal now is to buy a fuckload of Bitcoin, her home state of Michigan, and 6,000 swans simply because she can.

Connect with Branden at:

Facebook: Branden.Lanette

Instagram: @Brandenlanettel

Twitter: @Branden_LaNette

Visit Branden's website at:

OnceUponATimeBitches.com

About Andrea Waltz...

ANDREA is co-author of the best-selling book, *Go for No!* She teaches people how to reprogram the way they think about failure and rejection to be more successful.

Andrea is co-founder of Success In 100 Pages, the proud publisher of this book, and many great books, including three by co-author, Branden LaNette.

While she admits she is not a "crypto expert," Andrea believed that—together, with Branden—she could use her writing skills and publishing platform to share what she's learned about the current economy, looming financial crisis (and Bitcoin!) to help women understand this new world of cryptocurrencies—and take control of their financial future.

Connect with Andrea at:

Instagram: @GoForNo

Twitter: @GoForNo

Visit Andrea's website at:

GoForNo.com

That's it.

The book is over.

**Go buy some
Bitcoin.**